Amazing Science Discoveries

ASTRONOMY

The story of stars and galaxies

Dr. Bryson Gore

Stargazer Books

Mankato • Minnesota

CONTENTS

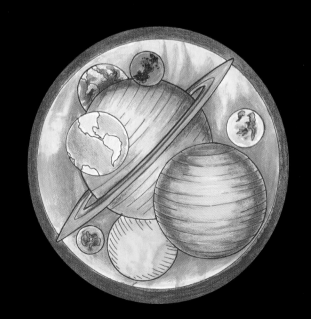

Designed and produced by
Aladdin Books Ltd

First published in 2009
in the United States by Stargazer Books,
distributed by Black Rabbit Books
P.O. Box 3263
Mankato, MN 56002

Printed in the United States

Editors: Katie Harker, Vivian Foster
Design: Flick, Book Design and Graphics
Illustrators: Q2A Creative

Picture research: Brian Hunter Smart

The author, Dr. Bryson Gore, is a freelance lecturer
and science demonstrator, working with the Royal
Institution and other science centers in the UK.

Library of Congress Cataloging-in-Publication Data

Gore, Bryson.
   Astronomy / Bryson Gore.
      p. cm. -- (Amazing science discoveries)
   Includes index.
   ISBN 978-1-59604-199-8
   1. Astronomy--Juvenile literature.
   2. Solar system--Juvenile literature. 3. Discoveries
in science--Juvenile literature I. Title.
   QB46.G729 2009
   520--dc22
                                       2008016501

Introduction

Humans have practiced ASTRONOMY—the science of space—for hundreds of thousands of years. From watching the stars we have discovered many things about our solar system—but many secrets of space are still waiting to be discovered.

In ancient times, astronomers could only look at the stars with the naked eye. The Greeks noticed points of light that appeared to move among the stars. They called these objects "planets." Later, we named these planets after Roman gods like Jupiter and Mars.

After the invention of the telescope in 1600 AD, people were able to observe details of space that had never been seen before.

By the 20th century, humans were not content to just guess at what was in space. They wanted to see it first-hand. The space rocket was invented. The first one just broke through Earth's gravity, but then rockets traveled to the moon and other planets. Since then satellites, space probes, space stations, and human-crewed expeditions have brought us a lot closer to understanding the universe.

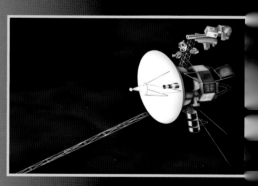

This book takes a look at twelve of the most amazing astronomical developments that have taken place throughout history. Find out about famous astronomers like William Herschel and Giovanni Cassini. Learn about our sun and its solar system, the planets and their moons, and the stars and galaxies.

By using the fact boxes, you will soon start to understand the wonder of our universe.

THE UNIVERSE BEGAN WITH A BIG BANG

Today, it is believed that the universe and all the ma... exploded out of just one tiny portion of space. This place around 10 to 15 billion years ago, and scienti... have named it the "Big Bang." The explosion happened in a fraction of a second. Astronomers believe that the explosion was so powerful that the universe is still expanding.

This theory has been supported by the discovery of a background that glows throughout space. Today, the glow is a color that we cannot see with the naked eye.

How do we know?

About 100 years ago, scientists began to measure how fast galaxies were moving, using the "Doppler Shift" (see page 7).

They learned that almost every galaxy is moving away from Earth. The farther away, the faster the galaxy was moving. Some were moving away at about 12,400 miles per second (20,000 km/s).

Have you noticed
how the sound of a police
siren changes as the car
approaches and then passes you?

This effect is called the Doppler Shift and it
occurs when a sound is generated by, or
reflected off, a moving object. This means
you hear a higher "note" as the car
approaches, but it will suddenly shift to a
lower note as the car passes.

The Doppler Shift holds for light,
too. That's how it shows the
movement of stars and
galaxies.

**Gravity is a force that causes
all objects in space to attract
each other.**

Will this force eventually become too
powerful and pull everything together?
Scientists call this the "Big Crunch."

OUR UNIVERSE CONTAINS OVER 100 BILLION GALAXIES

If you look at the sky on a clear night you can see thousands of stars twinkling above you. Did you know that you can also see six or seven galaxies? Scientists believe that the universe contains as many as 100 billion galaxies.

How do we know?

Most galaxies are too far away for us to see without a telescope.

Nobody has ever counted the total number of stars and galaxies in the universe—there are just too many!

Astronomers, however, have counted how many stars and galaxies there are in lots of small areas. By doing this, they have been able to estimate the total number in the universe. Of course, this is only assuming that the rest of the sky that is not visible has a similar number.

1

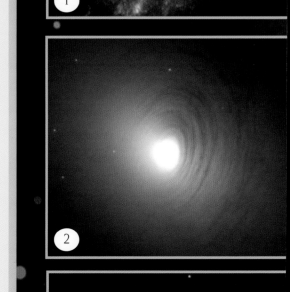

2

3

Stars and galaxies were formed after the Big Bang when the force of gravity pulled clouds of gas and dust together.

The earth and the sun are located inside a common spiral galaxy, the "Milky Way." The Milky Way is part of a cluster of six or seven galaxies.

The nearest galaxy cluster to us is about 50 million light-years away. The pull of gravity causes the shapes of galaxies we can see.

There are three basic types of galaxies:
Our galaxy—the Milky Way—is a **spiral galaxy (1)**. These consist of large flat disks and young star clusters.

Elliptical galaxies (2) are formed when spiral galaxies collide.
Irregular galaxies (3) are formed when one galaxy nearly collides with another.

EVERY GALAXY HAS A BLACK HOLE AT ITS CENTER

The universe is full of galaxies. These are collections of gas, dust, and billions of stars that have been drawn together by the effect of gravity. However, the pull of gravity causes the galaxies to collapse, leaving a big "black hole" in the center—just like water being dragged down a drain.

The science of . . .

Black holes are possibly the strangest objects in the universe.

They are regions of space where gravity is so powerful that even light cannot escape. Although they are called holes, they are anything but empty! They contain enormous amounts of compressed matter.

Some black holes form after a very large star uses up all its fuel and blows off its outer parts in an enormous explosion, called a supernova. What remains is a highly compressed and extremely large core.

WOWZSAT!

Our own star, the sun, is too small to end up as a black hole. It would only form a black hole if it were squeezed into a tiny space just 3.7 miles (6 km) across.

How do we Know?

Because light rays cannot escape the immense pull of gravity in a black hole, we will never be able to see them.

Scientists are confident they exist because of the strange behavior of matter we see near a black hole. For example, a star might "wobble" or spin for no visible reason. Or gases might swirl around these regions.

Astronomers now believe this could be due to the gravity of a nearby black hole.

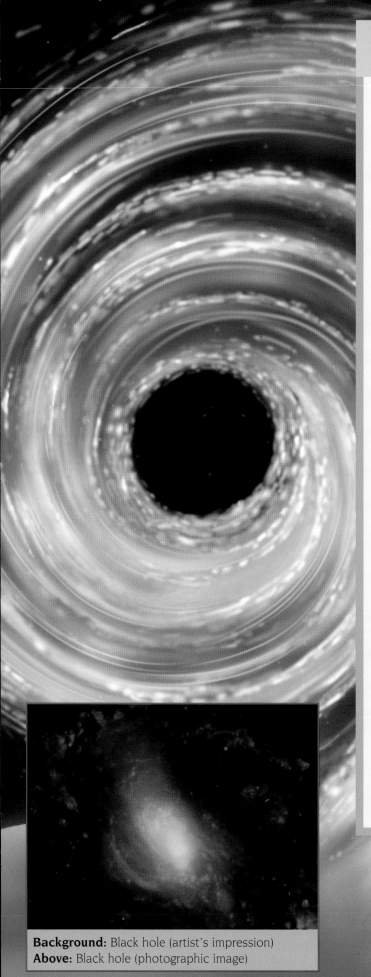

Background: Black hole (artist's impression)
Above: Black hole (photographic image)

THE CENTER OF THE SUN IS OVER 27 MILLION °F (15 MILLION °C)

That is very, very hot! So hot in fact, that it is difficult to imagine what it must be like. Why is the sun the hottest natural object in the solar system?

1. 10,800 °F (6,000 °C) = SURFACE OF THE SUN
2. 43,000 °F (24,000 °C) = LIGHTNING BOLT
3. 27,000,000°F (15,000,000 °C) = NUCLEAR EXPLOSION

1.

2.

The science of . . .

The sun is a star—
a spinning ball of hot gas
about 1.3 million times bigger
than Earth.

The sun formed about 4.6 billion years ago when a cloud of gas (mostly helium and hydrogen) started to collapse due to gravity. High pressure in the center of this ball of cloud caused the temperature to rise to about 27 million °F (15 million °C). This was hot enough to start a nuclear reaction.

These reactions convert hydrogen to helium which creates enormous energy. Most of this energy is released as heat.

WOWZSAT!

Is it possible the sun could just burn out? This is possible, but at the moment it is burning nuclear fuel at a steady rate, so we have about four billion years left!

How do we Know?

Astronomers cannot go to the sun and measure its heat directly—no space probe would survive the extreme temperatures.

Instead, they determine the heat by taking measurements of sunlight and using mathematical equations. They have estimated that for a ball of gas the size of our sun, the pressure at the center is 250 billion times greater than that of our own atmosphere.

3.

The sun's heat provides Earth with the ideal conditions for life. Other planets are too cold or too hot, with the exception of Mars (*below*).

Betelgeuse is one of the stars in the constellation of Orion (*below*). Betelgeuse is a "Red Giant." It is about 500 times bigger than our own sun and has a surface temperature of 5,400 °F (3,000 °C) .

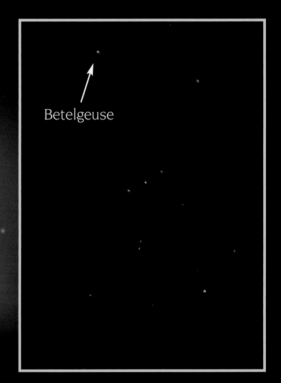

Betelgeuse

YOU CAN TELL HOW HOT A STAR IS BY LOOKING AT ITS COLOR

At first, astronomers were interested in the brightness of stars and their location. Then, about 100 years ago, they discovered they could measure their temperature and how fast the stars were moving.

How do we Know?

Over 100 years ago, scientists realized that light is a type of heat, or energy.

Light is a type of wave that can travel across space, and gives off a color measured in nanometers.

The main color given off by an object has a wavelength that is proportional to its temperature. The color of the sun tells us that it has a surface temperature of about 10,800°F (6,000°C). In comparison a candle flame is about 2,200°F (1,200°C).

The science of . . .

Any material will glow and give out light if you heat it up, whatever its normal color.

The hotter an object gets, the brighter it becomes, and the light also becomes bluer. Blue/white hot is hotter than red hot!

Smaller stars tend to be colder, dimmer, and redder. Heavier stars tend to be hotter, brighter, and bluer in color. These "Blue Giants" are much bigger than our sun and have a surface heat of 36,000°F (20,000°C).

JUPITER IS LIKE A STAR THAT FAILED TO IGNITE

About 5 billion years ago, an area of gas at the edge of a spiral galaxy began to collapse as the force of gravity pulled it together. Because the gas was rotating it began to flatten and spin faster, forming a disk. This disk clumped together and formed the planets in our solar system.

The science of . . .

Jupiter, Saturn, Uranus, and Neptune are planets called "gas giants."

They are great globes of dense gas that have little or no rocky material. These planets are virtually all atmosphere, with Jupiter being the largest.

Jupiter is made from a very similar mix of atoms to our sun. Jupiter has a small rocky core that is covered by solid hydrogen. If Jupiter had 100 times more mass, it would have turned into a star like our sun.

Uranus has an atmosphere composed of mostly hydrogen.

How do we know?

Computers can show exactly how our solar system was formed. Starting with hundreds of millions of atoms, we can ask the computer to work out what would happen over millions of years.

Depending on how the atoms begin their journey, the computer can show different sorts of solar systems. All solar systems have at least one star at the center where most of the atoms collect.

Sometimes the system forms two stars that orbit each other; these are called binary stars. About half the stars in the sky are binary stars.

WOWZSAT!

Did you know that Jupiter is so big that all the other planets in our solar system could fit inside it? If it were any bigger it might become too hot and turn into a sun.

17

WE ARE ALL MADE OF STARDUST

Your body is made up of dozens of different kinds of atoms such as hydrogen, oxygen, carbon, and iron. The earth is also made from a similar selection of atoms, but where did they all come from?

The Big Bang created lots of light gases like hydrogen and helium. For billions of years, stars have been making heavier atoms like carbon and iron by squeezing the lighter atoms together.

The science of . . .

Scientists believe that heavier atoms like gold and silver were made in a series of gigantic explosions (or supernovae), releasing debris we call "nebulae."

When large stars die, they explode and release heavy atoms. Atoms like these mixed with hydrogen gas in space, and cooled to form the ball of gas that collapsed to form our sun and the planets.

It is estimated that it took around 200 million years for the earth to form in this way.

A supernova (*above*). Gaseous pillars of the Eagle Nebula (*bottom*)

How do we know?

All the matter in the universe was present in the Big Bang. It only formed into atoms a few minutes later. Before that the universe was just too hot.

Computers have shown that roughly three minutes after the Big Bang, the universe had cooled enough to produce four new, light atoms—helium, lithium, beryllium, and boron.

We now know that all atoms that are lighter than iron originate from stars. All atoms that are heavier than iron came from exploding stars. When dust from a supernova mixes with gas, the heavier atoms collide and—over millions of years—start to form larger and larger clumps of rocks.

WOWZSAT!

Supernovae were very common when the universe was more dense. When the sun formed, the universe was nearly four times as dense as it is now.

19

THE EARTH WEIGHS ABOUT SIX BILLION, TRILLION TONS

Have you ever traveled in an airplane and looked down from the window? If so, you will probably have been amazed at the immense size of planet Earth. It has a circumference of 24,855 miles (40,000 km) and a surface area of 190 million square miles (0.5 billion square km). It is also very heavy.

6,000,000,000,000,000,000,000 tonnes

The science of . . .

Even though the earth has a mass of six billion, trillion tons, in fact it weighs nothing at all!

Although on Earth mass and weight mean almost the same thing, in space they are very different. Mass tells us how hard it is to make something move. Weight is the force by which an object is pulled downward, and is measured in newtons (N).

An object may have a mass of 2.2 lb (1 kg), but in space it would not push down on a weighing scale.

Scientists have discovered that the earth is so heavy because it has a core of iron.

How do we know?

Gravitational constant (G) was first measured by Henry Cavendish in 1798.

We know that everything pulls on everything else in a simple way that involves only mass and distance. Using this knowledge, Cavendish measured the force of gravity between two balls of lead and calculated the value of "G." He then went on to use this knowledge to calculate the mass of the earth.

How do we know?

Because we can now send satellites into space, it is possible to find out far more about a planet's geographical features.

For example, we have discovered a lot about Mars because there is so little atmosphere hiding its surface.

Using a probe called Mars Global Surveyor, scientists have found that Mars has almost all the geographical features we see on Earth. Although it is believed there was once water on this planet, today it is only in the form of ice.

In 1969, a physicist called Weisskopf asked himself whether there was a limit to a mountain's height. He estimated that if a mountain grew too tall, its weight would melt the rocks at its base.

To compare the mountain on Mars with one on Earth, Mauna Kea on the island of Hawaii is 6 miles (10 km) tall, compared to Olympus Mons at 15 miles (24 km) tall.

THE TALLEST KNOWN VOLCANO IS ON MARS

Olympus Mons is the largest mountain in the solar system. It can be found on the planet Mars, and its base measures more than 300 miles (500 km) in diameter. How did astronomers ever discover this monstrosity?

Earth is thought to be the planet with the most volcanoes in our solar system.

The reason Earth has more geological activity is due to the combination of heat and water making the rocks less dense.

Other planets have active mountains, too. A range of volcanoes, known as Maxwell Montes, have been discovered on Venus.

Io, a moon of Jupiter, also has active volcanoes that throw sulfur over 248 miles (400 km) into space.

Olympus Mons as seen from space (*top left*) with three smaller volcanoes known as the Tharsis triple.

23

IF YOU COULD DRIVE TO THE SUN IT WOULD TAKE 200 YEARS

Everyone knows that the sun is a really long way away. But how far away is the sun, and how on earth do we measure this vast distance?

The universe is so vast that we are unable to measure it accurately in miles. We don't know the exact size of the universe, but even if you could travel across it at the speed of light, it would take at least 15 billion years to cross it!

How do we know?

If you hold your thumb at arm's-length and close one eye at a time, you will see that your thumb moves against the background of distant objects. This effect is called "parallax."

Having first worked out the distance of Earth from Mars, Cassini used trigonometry to assess that Earth was about 90 million miles (150 million km) from the sun.

A scientist called Cassini used this simple trick to measure the distance from the earth to the sun.

Today, astronomers use a similar method to calculate the earth–sun distance, but instead of using Mars they use the planet Venus.

The science of . . .

How long would it take to get to the sun?

- Riding a bicycle, it would take you about 1,000 years to reach the sun, at 15 feet (5 meters) per second.
- A car traveling at 80 ft/s (25 m/s) would take 200 years. A racing car traveling at 160 ft/s (50 m/s) would take 100 years.
- A supersonic jet traveling at 1,600 ft/s (500 m/s) would take over 10 years.
- Even light takes about 8 minutes to get from the sun to the earth, and that travels at 186,000 mi/s (300 million m/s).

PLANET	AVERAGE DISTANCE TO THE SUN
Mercury	36 million miles (58m km)
Venus	67 million miles (108m km)
Earth	93 million miles (150m km)
Mars	142 million miles (228m km)
Jupiter	483 million miles (778m km)
Saturn	886 million miles (1,427m km)
Uranus	1,784 million miles (2,871m km)
Neptune	2,794 million miles (4,497m km)
Pluto	3,674 million miles (5,913m km)

Pluto is now a minor planet.

MANMADE OBJECTS ARE NOW EXPLORING BEYOND THE SOLAR SYSTEM

Humans have always loved exploring. In the 20th century, space travel became possible. As space probes were sent up into the sky to explore the planets, men and women ventured into the depths of space itself.

The science of . . .

The modern space age began in 1957 when the Soviet Union launched the first satellite, Sputnik 1.

Within two years, unmanned spacecraft were sent to the moon. By the end of the 1960s, astronauts had actually walked on the moon.

Many probes are still orbiting the planets. They send back information to Earth via radio telescopes.

In the 1980s, the space shuttle began to ferry people and equipment to and from space.

WOWZSAT!

It is thought that over one million pieces of junk could be orbiting the earth. Objects the size of postage stamps are believed to be fragments of manmade satellites.

26

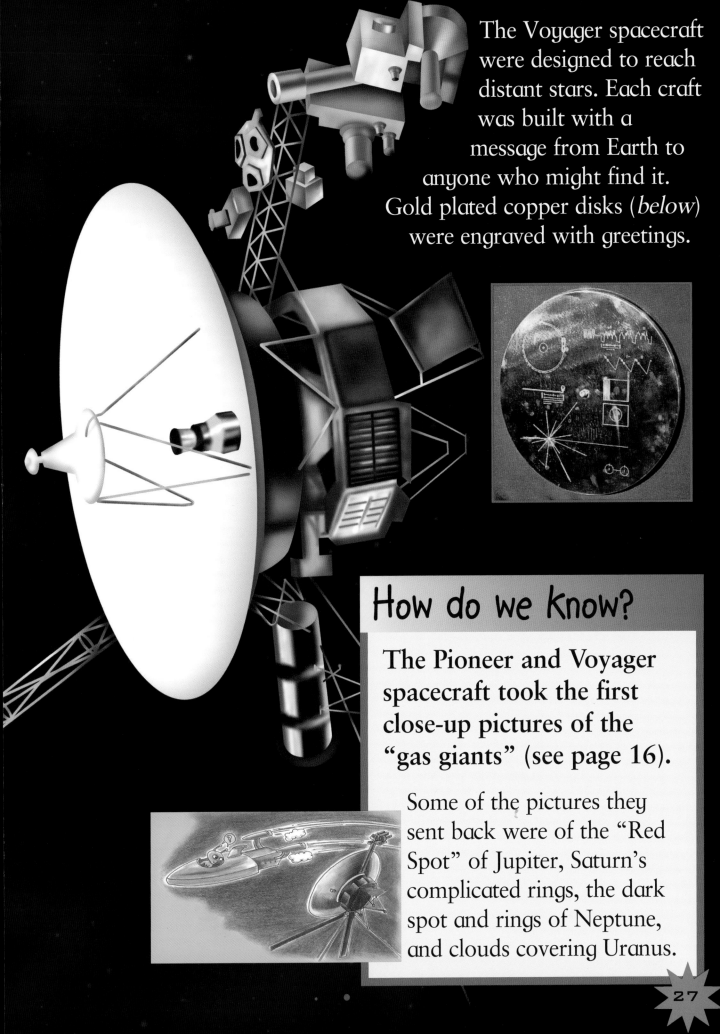

The Voyager spacecraft were designed to reach distant stars. Each craft was built with a message from Earth to anyone who might find it. Gold plated copper disks (*below*) were engraved with greetings.

How do we know?

The Pioneer and Voyager spacecraft took the first close-up pictures of the "gas giants" (see page 16).

Some of the pictures they sent back were of the "Red Spot" of Jupiter, Saturn's complicated rings, the dark spot and rings of Neptune, and clouds covering Uranus.

IN 2004 SCIENTISTS DISCOVERED ANOTHER PLANET ORBITING THE SUN

In March 2004, U.S. scientists announced the discovery of a new planet orbiting the sun. They named the planet Sedna, after the Innuit goddess of the sea. This discovery highlighted the fact that we still know so little about the universe.

The science of . . .

In the last decade, scientists have discovered about 800 objects located beyond the orbit of Neptune. Sedna was one of the larger ones.

But is Sedna really a planet? It is certainly big enough with a diameter of 1,056 miles (1,700 km). It is in a region of space surrounding the sun, called the Oort cloud. This area is incredibly cold. It is estimated that rocks in the Oort cloud could be colder than –420°F (–250°C)

28

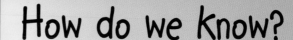

Uranus was discovered when William Herschel saw a disk of light through his telescope.

Sedna was discovered by chance when astronomers were studying objects on the edge of the solar system. Sedna appeared as a moving dot of light.

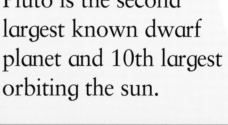

Pluto is the second largest known dwarf planet and 10th largest orbiting the sun.

Mercury, Venus, Mars, Jupiter, and Saturn can all be seen with the naked eye. Uranus was discovered in 1781. Neptune was officially recognized as a planet in 1846. Pluto was discovered in 1930.

Glossary

Astronomer—A scientist who studies the universe.

Atmosphere—The gas that surrounds a planet.

Atom—The smallest piece of a pure chemical element.

Black hole—A massive star that has collapsed.

Doppler Shift—The change in pitch of sound, or in the color of light, given out by a moving object.

Fusion—The process by which lighter atoms are combined to make heavier ones.

Gravity—The force that pulls all materials together across space.

Light-year—The distance traveled by light, through space, in one year.

Nanometer (nm)—A nanometer is one millionth of a millimeter.

Orbit—The path of an object as it travels around another object.

Planet—A large ball of gas or rock that orbits a star.

Radar—A technique used for measuring the distance or speed of an object by measuring the echo of a radio wave.

Radio wave—A low-energy form of light that we cannot see with our eyes.

Space probe—A spacecraft that is designed to measure properties of the universe.

Star—A large ball of gas (mainly hydrogen and helium).

Supernova—The massive explosion that occurs when stars bigger than our sun have burned most of their hydrogen.

Telescope—A device for making far-away objects look larger and brighter.

Universe—Absolutely everything that exists, including us.

Weight—The force with which something is attracted to the earth.

Biography

Giovanni Cassini (1625–1712) An Italian astronomer who calculated the earth to sun distance.

Henry Cavendish (1731–1810) A British physicist who worked out the mass of the earth by measuring the gravitational constant ("G").

Christian Doppler (1803-1853) An Austrian physicist who is most famous for the Doppler Shift.

William Herschel (1738-1822) A British astronomer who discovered Uranus in 1781.

Sir Isaac Newton (1642-1727) A British scientist and mathematician famous for his theories on gravity.

Victor Weisskopf (1908-2002) An Austrian physicist who used physics to calculate things like the maximum height of a mountain.

KEY DATES

1608—The telescope is invented.
1781—Herschel discovers Uranus.
1923—Edwin Hubble discovers galaxies outside the Milky Way.
1957—Sputnik I becomes the first object to orbit the earth.
1961—Yuri Gagarin is the first man to orbit the earth.
1969—Neil Armstrong and Edwin Aldrin walk on the moon.

1976—The U.S. Viking probes land on Mars.
1981—The space shuttle is invented.
2004—The discovery of another planet, Sedna, is announced.
2006—Pluto is reclassified as a minor planet.

Index

Photocredits: Abbreviations: l-left, r-right, b-bottom, t-top, c-center, m-middle
Front cover l, back cover r, 8-9, 16br, 18 both, 26mr — Corbis. 1, 8mrt, 11bl, 16-17, 25tl, 31bl — NASA. 4mr, 7br, 13br, 23bl — Courtesy NASA/JPL - Caltech. 8mrb, 8br — NASA and The Hubble Heritage Team. 14mr — NASA Johnson Space Center - Earth Sciences and Image Analysis (NASA-JSC-ES&IA). 20-21, 31br — Flick Smith. 27mr — NASA/NSSDC.